PENGUIN BOOKS

ON READING

André Kertész was born in 1894 in Hungary, where he began taking pictures when he was sixteen. Self-taught and Ignorant of photographic fashions in the rest of the world, he became the unintentional inventor of what is now called the "candid" manner and produced during his service with the Austro-Hungarian army some of his greatest masterpieces. In 1925 he moved to Paris, joining in the life of the cafés and the boulevards, meeting and photographing painters and writers, presenting (in 1927) the first one-man photographic exhibition ever held, and pioneering in photojournalism. He later said. "Paris accepted me. After my first one-man show I felt at home. This is the biggest thing an artist can have." His reception in America, where he moved in 1936, was different if not positively hostile. In New York City, editors told him, "Your pictures talk too much," and for more than twenty years he was obliged to earn his living as a free-lance magazine photographer. Though American recognition was slow in coming, it did eventually arrive, culminating in his 1964 one-man show at New York's Museum of Modern Art. Mr. Kertész has published many books of photographs, including *André Kertész: Sixty Years of Photography, J'aime Paris,* and *Washington Square.*

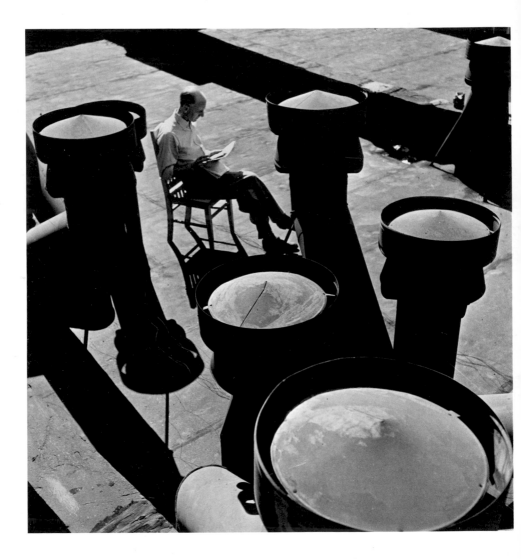

ON READING

ANDRÉ KERTÉSZ

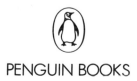

PENGUIN BOOKS

To my brothers

Penguin Books Ltd, Harmondsworth,
Middlesex, England
Penguin Books, 625 Madison Avenue,
New York, New York 10022, U.S.A.
Penguin Books Australia Ltd, Ringwood,
Victoria, Australia
Penguin Books Canada Limited, 2801 John Street,
Markham, Ontario, Canada L3R 1B4
Penguin Books (N.Z.) Ltd, 182—190 Wairau Road,
Auckland 10, New Zealand

First published in the United States of America by
Grossman Publishers 1971
First published in Canada by
The Macmillan Company of Canada Limited 1971
Viking Compass Edition published 1975
Published in Penguin Books 1982

LIBRARY OF CONGRESS CATALOGING IN PUBLICATION DATA
Kertész, André.
On reading.
Reprint. Originally published: New York: Grossman, 1971.
1. Photography, Artistic. 2. Kertész, André.
I. Title.
[TR654.K45   1982]   779'.9028'0924   82-7551
ISBN 0 14 00.6309 9   AACR2

Printed in the United States of America by
Rapoport Printing Corp. in the Stonetone process

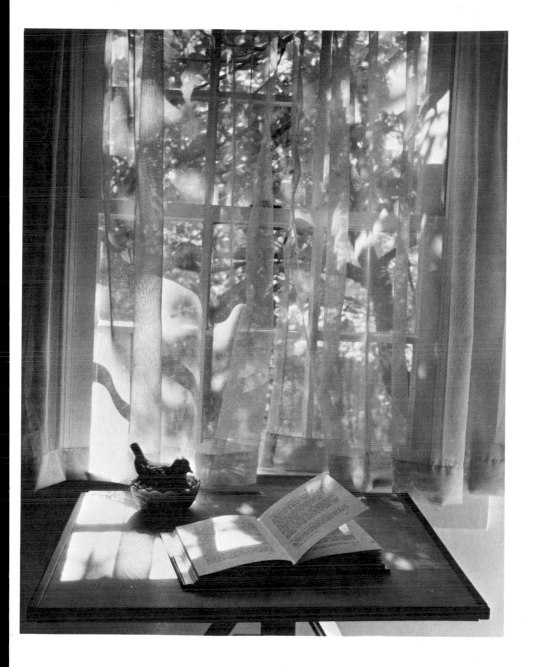

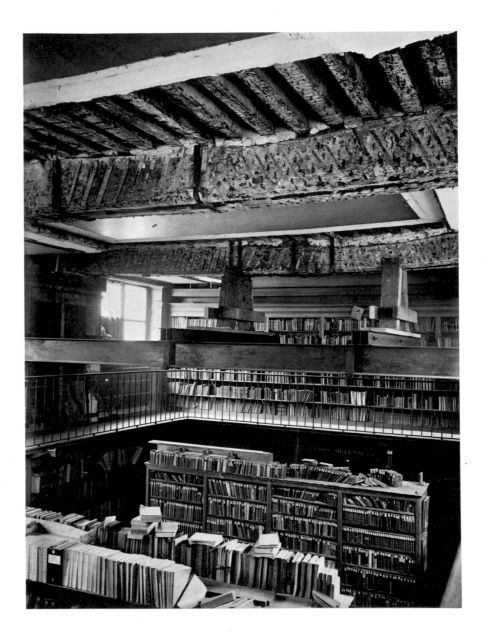

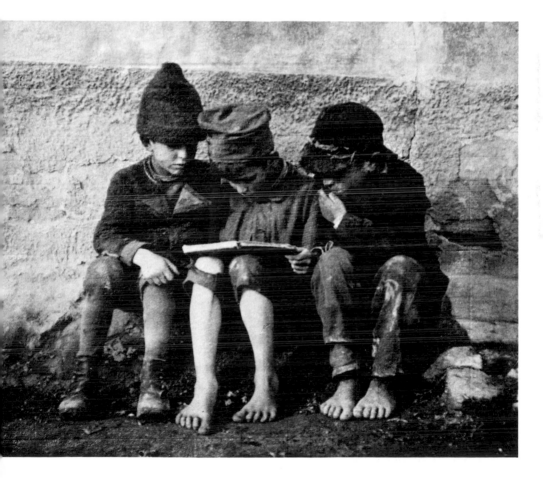

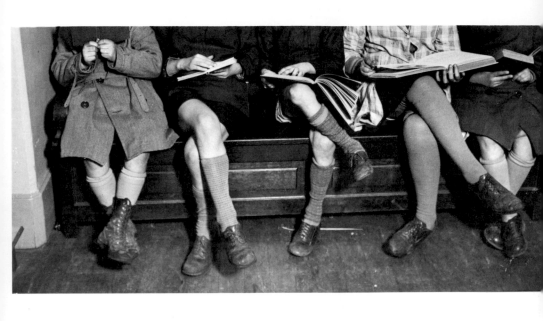

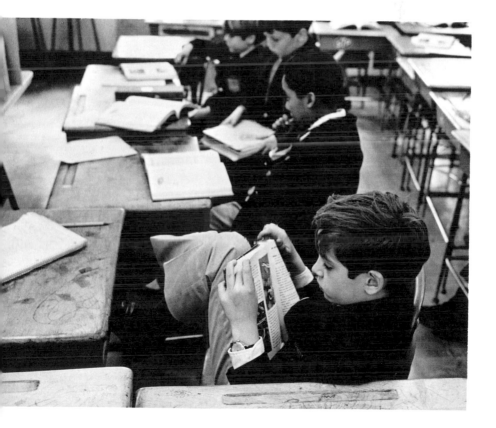

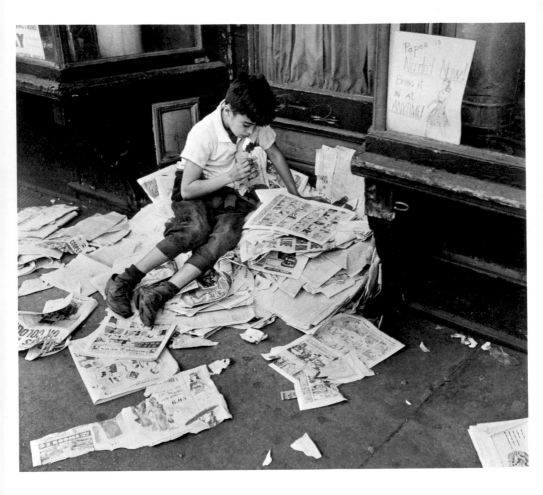

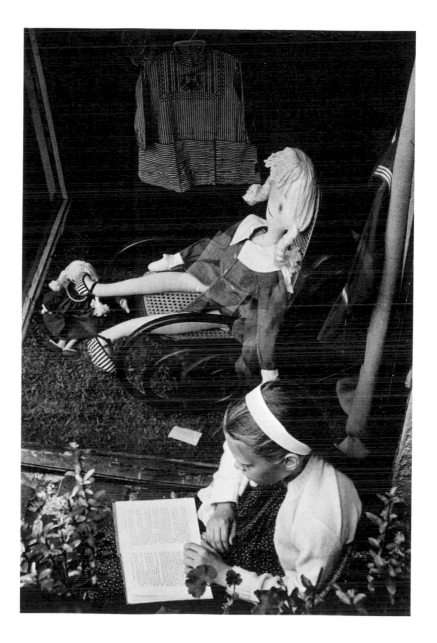

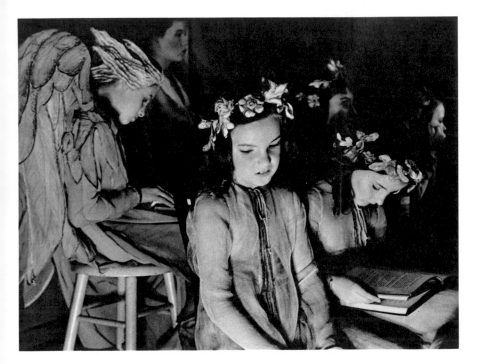

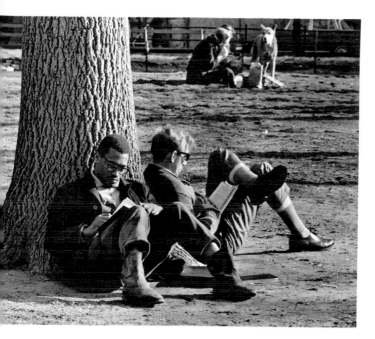

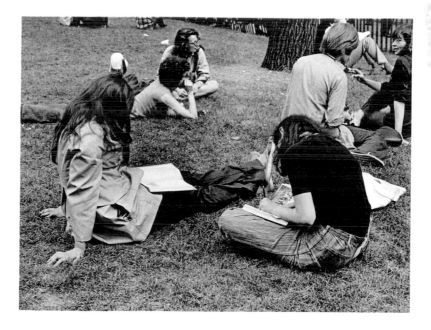

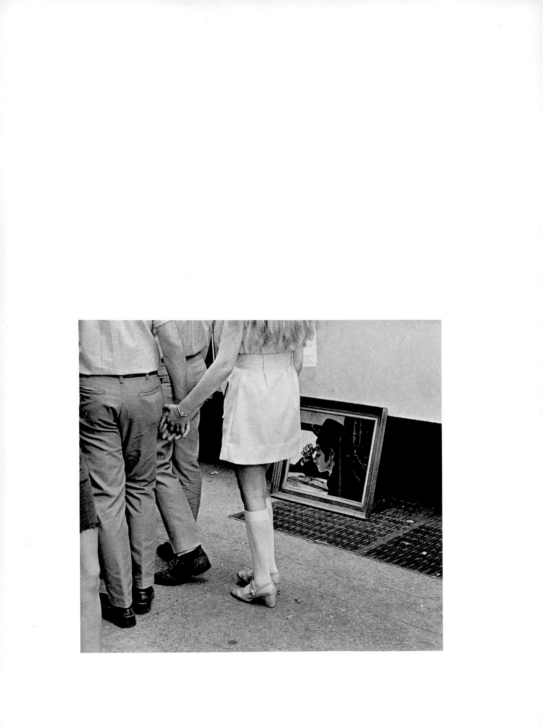

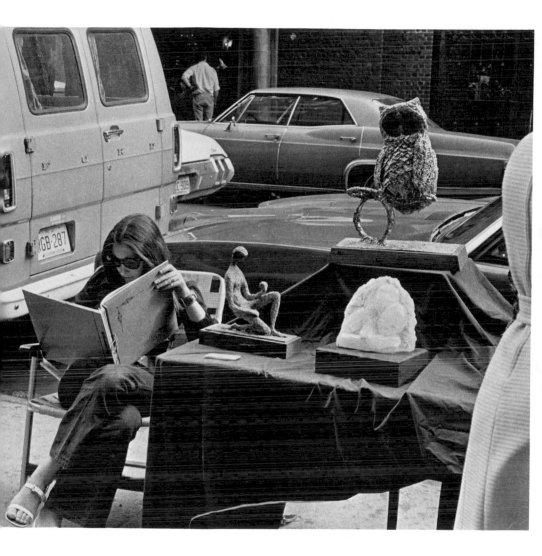

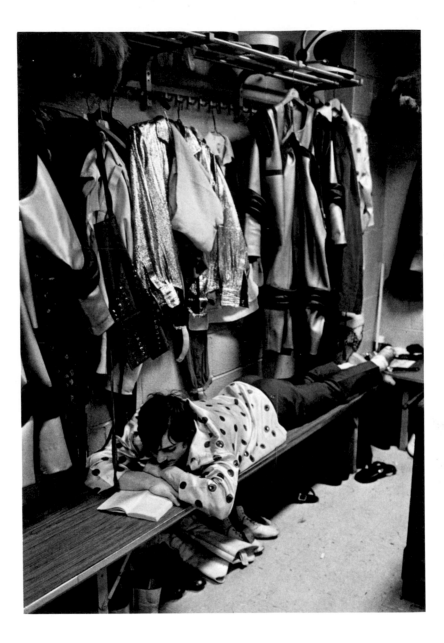

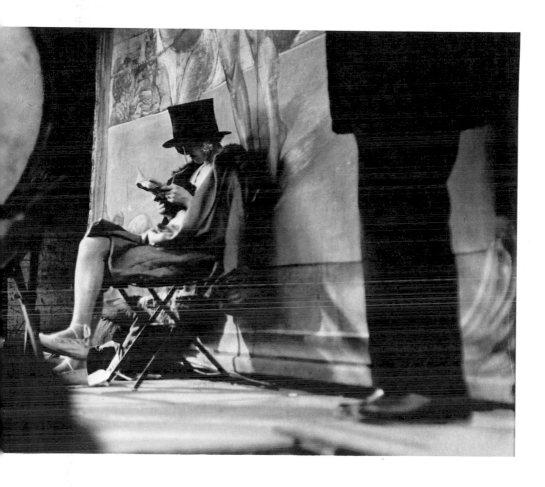

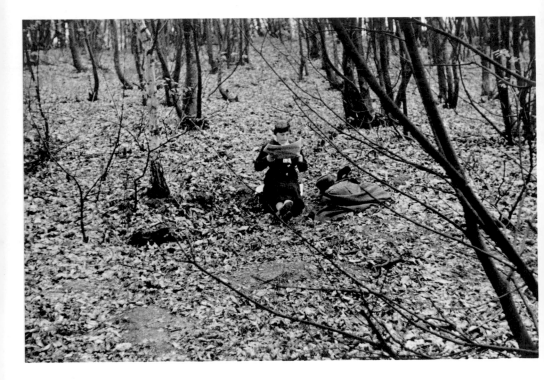

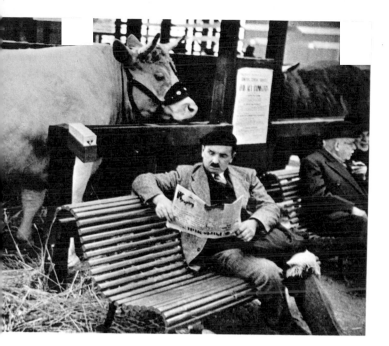

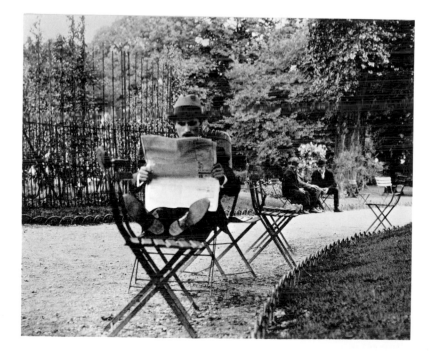

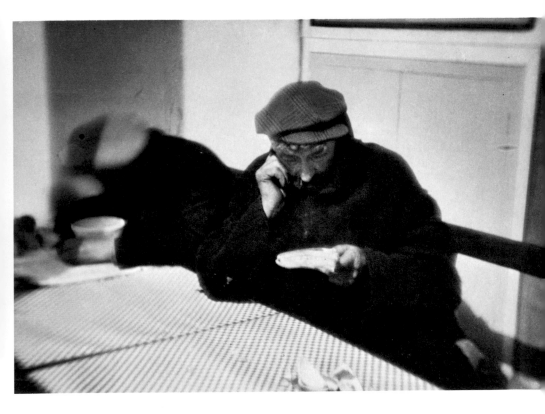

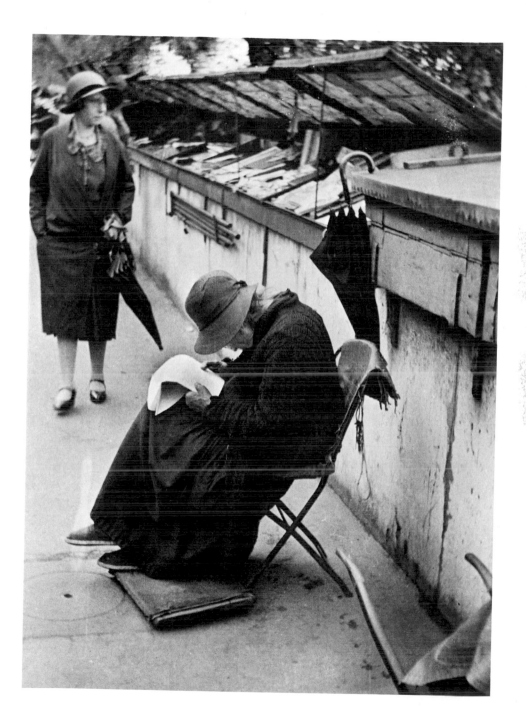

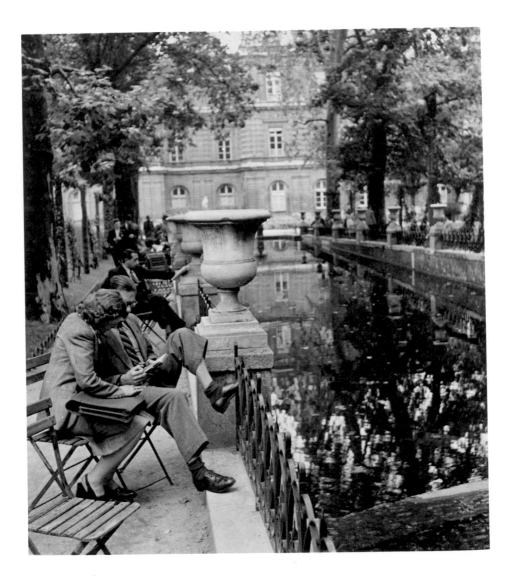

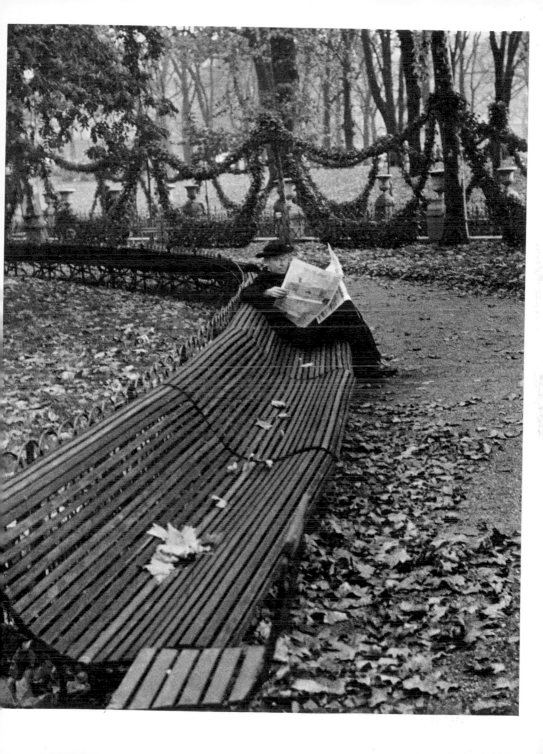

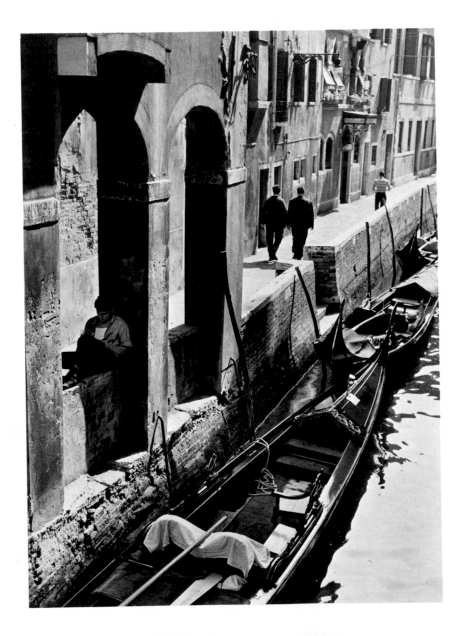

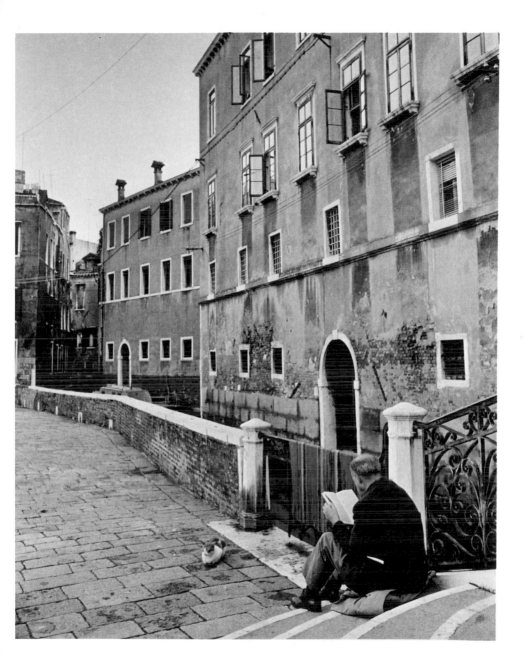

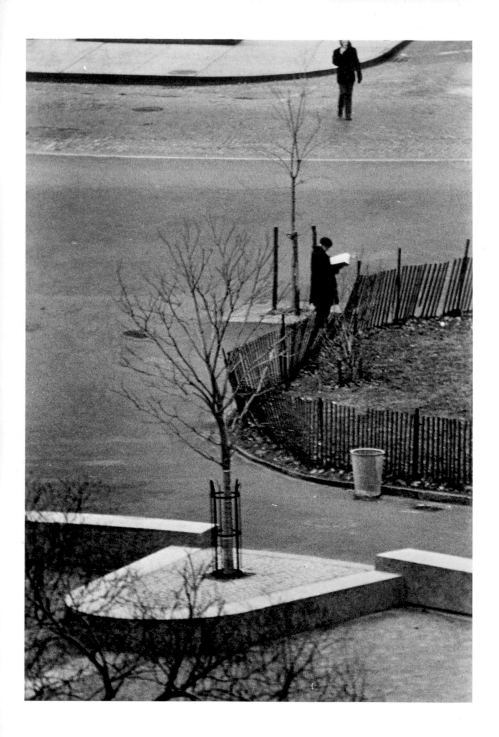

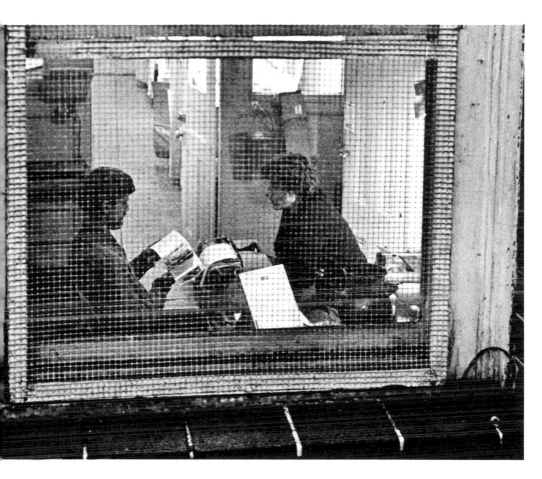

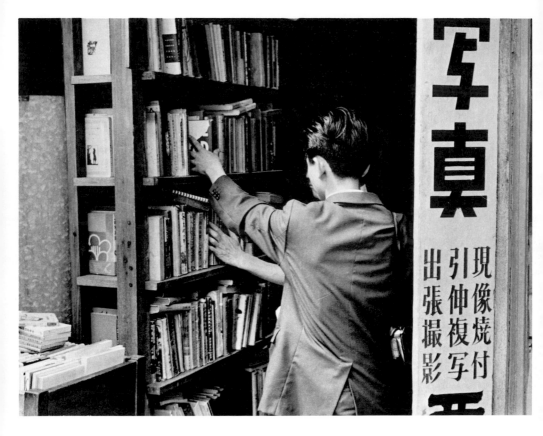

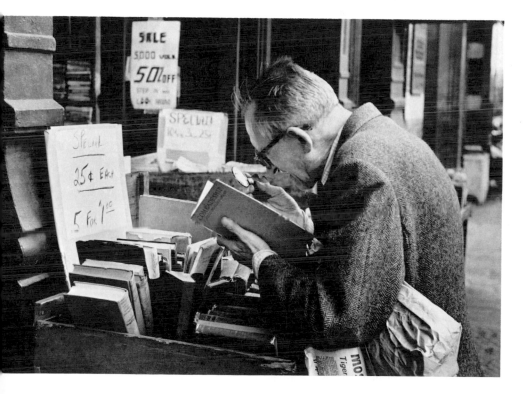

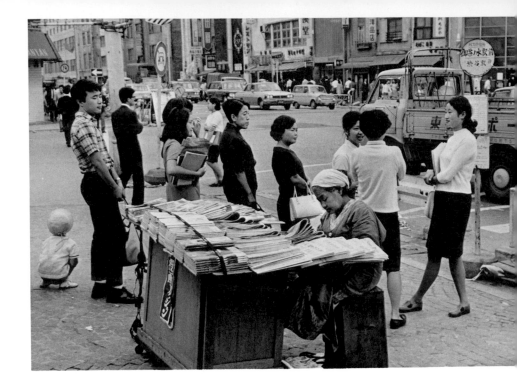

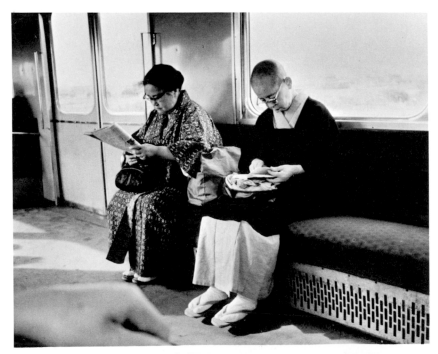

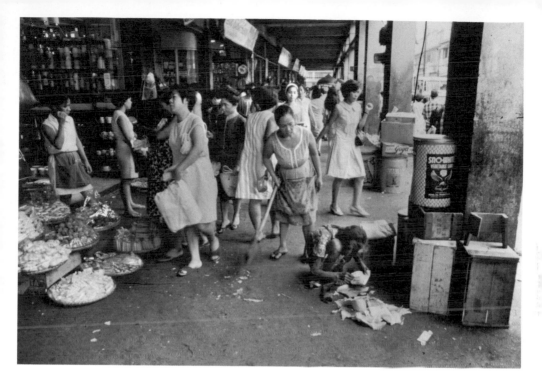

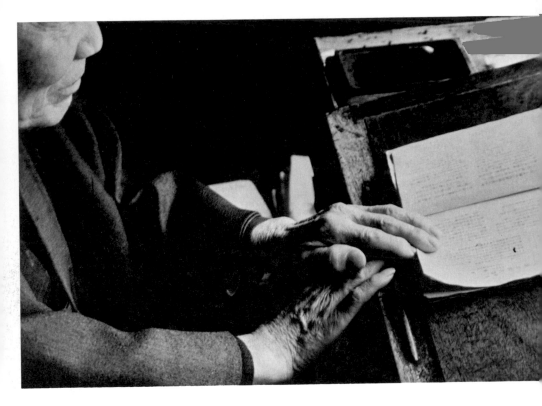

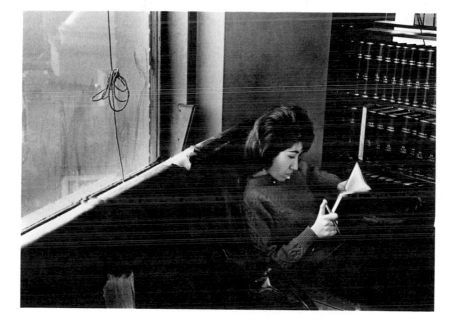

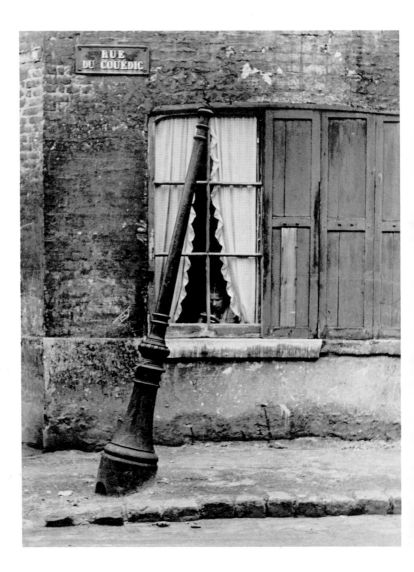

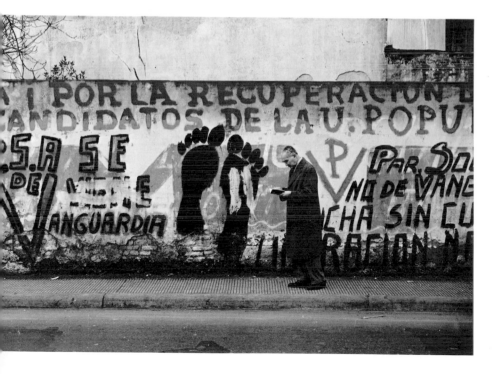

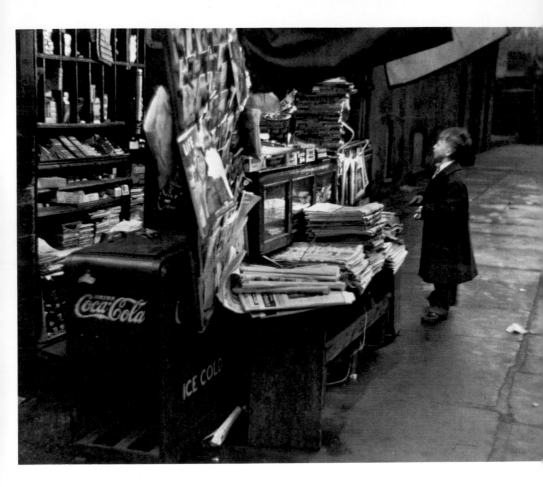

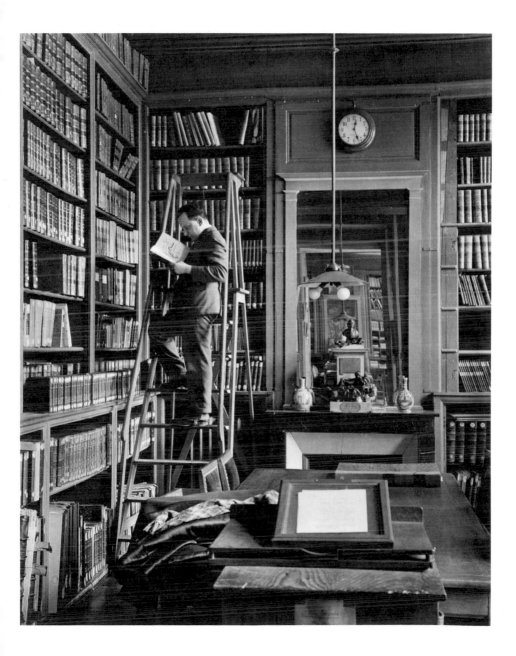

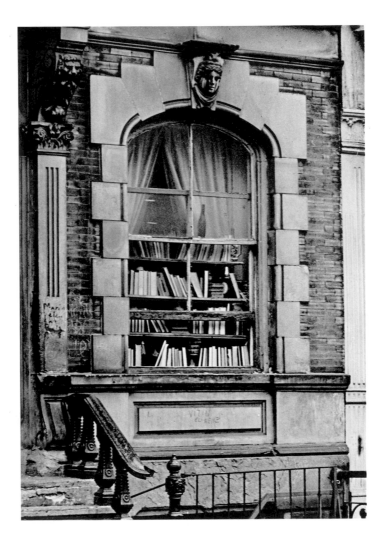

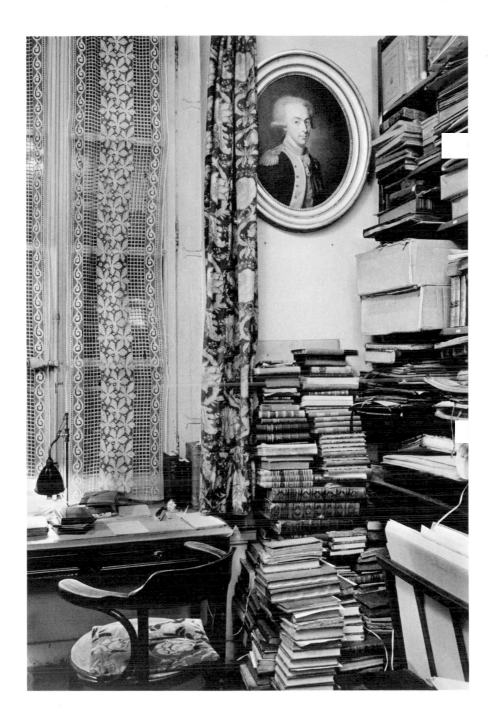

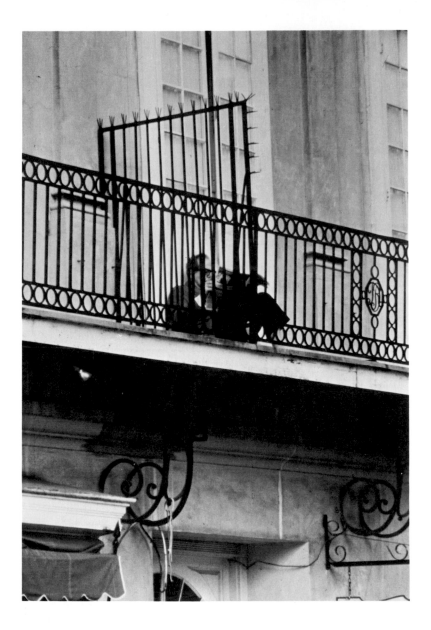

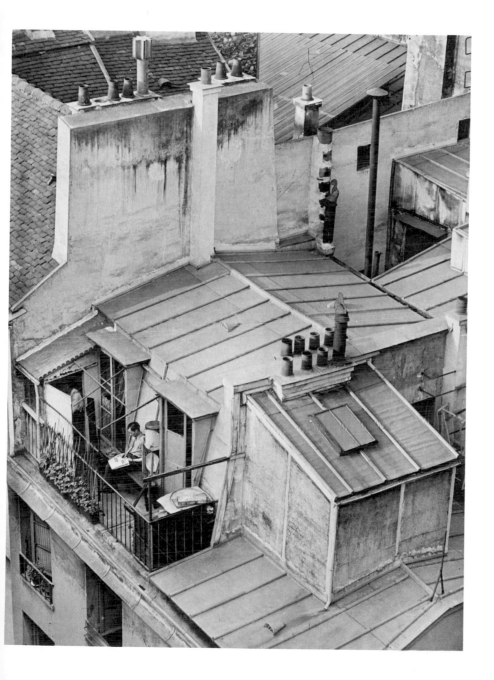

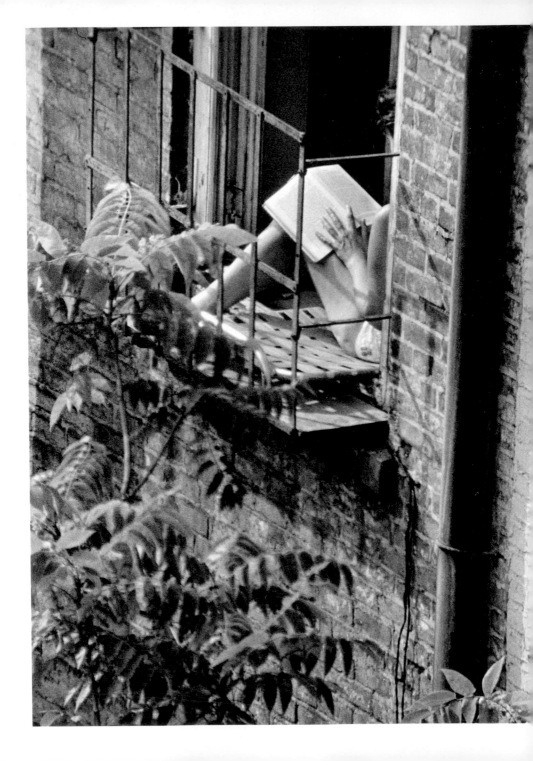

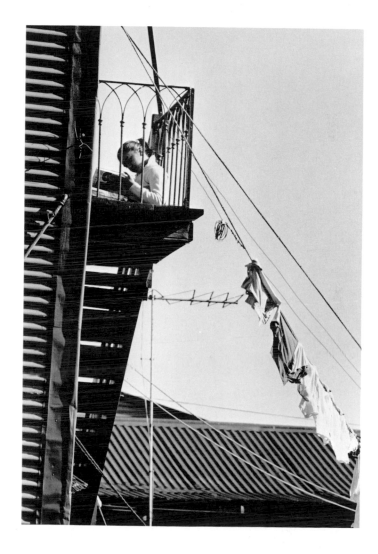

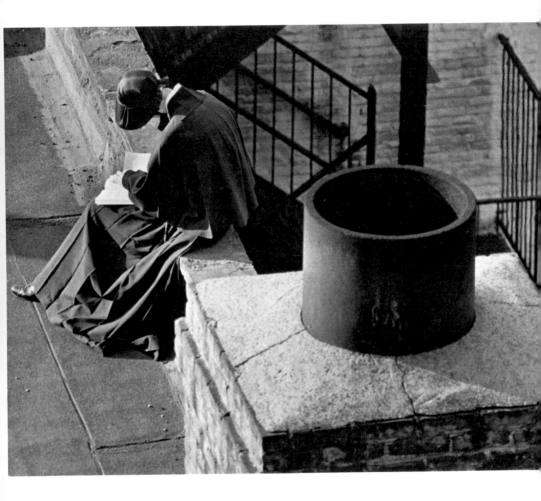

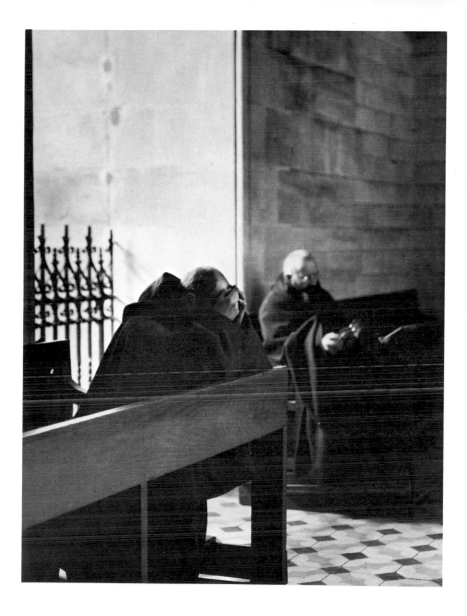

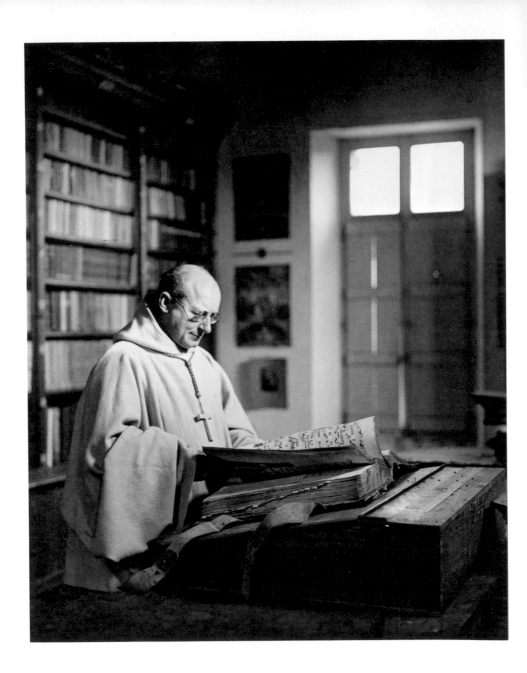

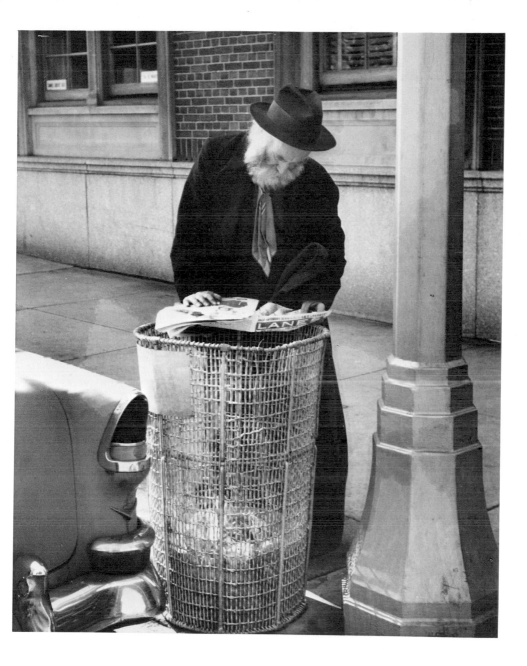

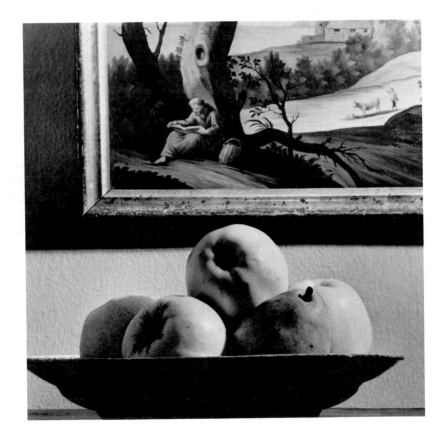

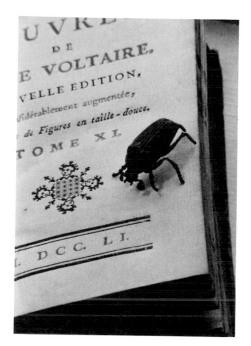

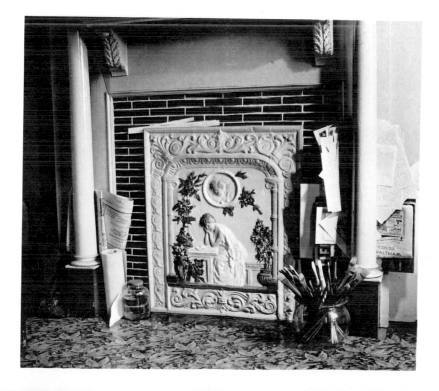

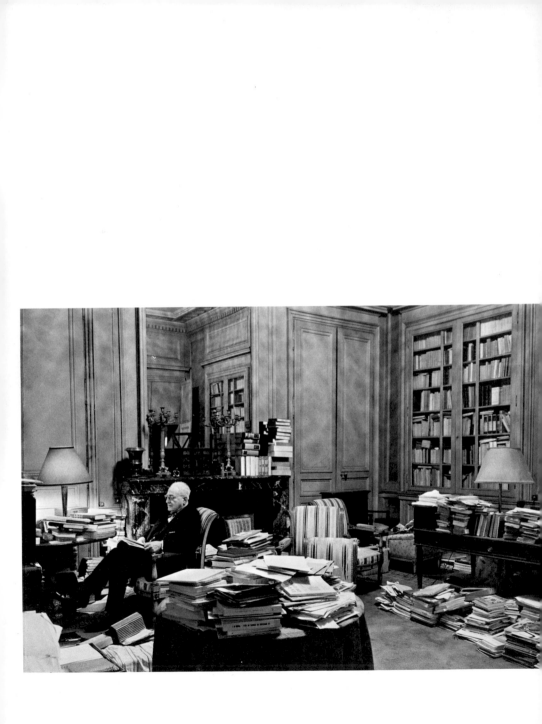

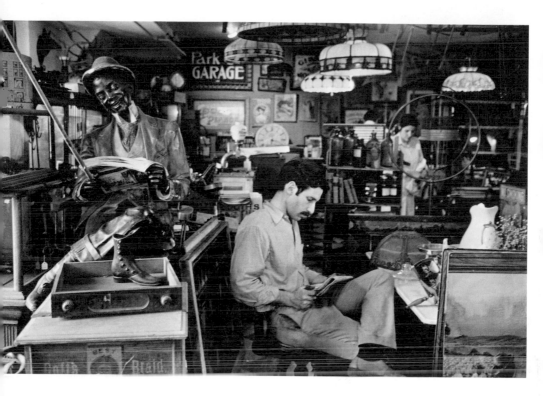

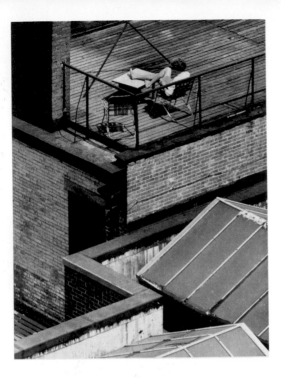

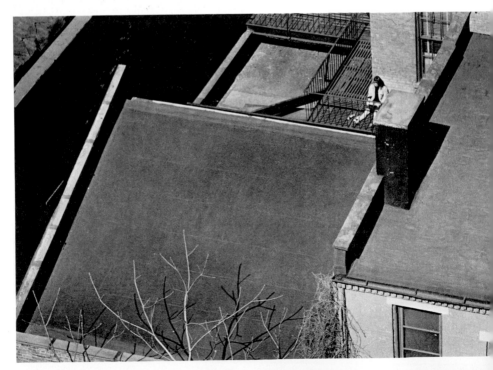

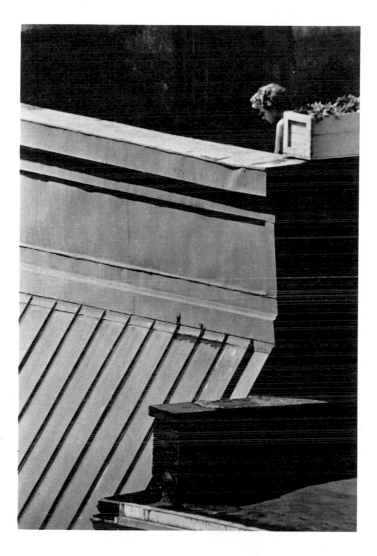

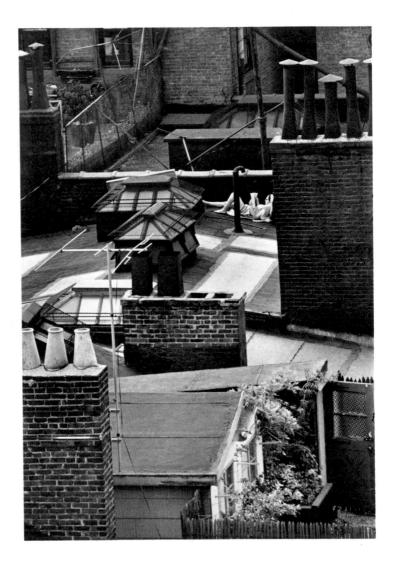

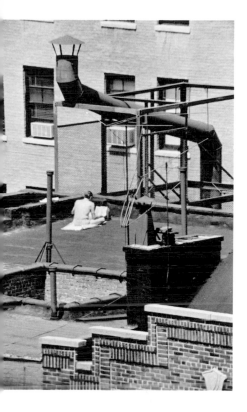

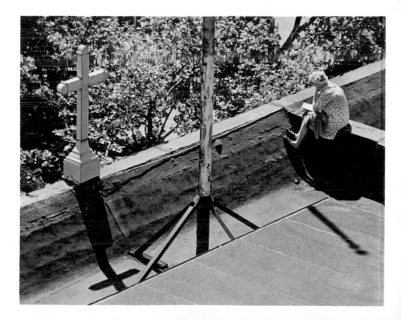

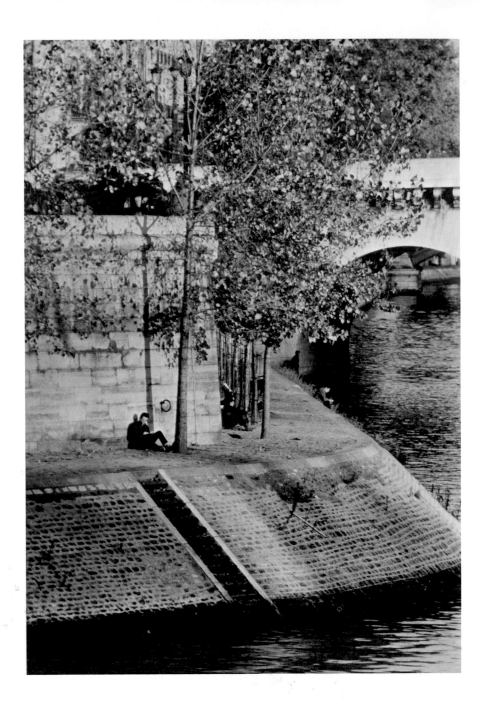

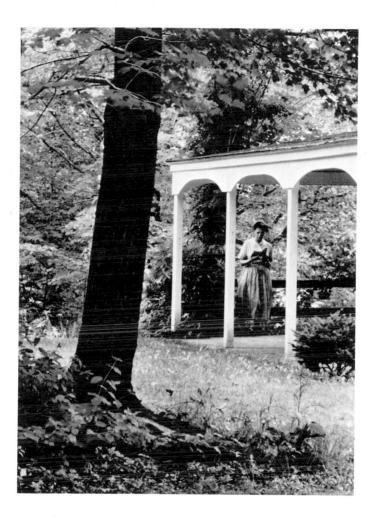

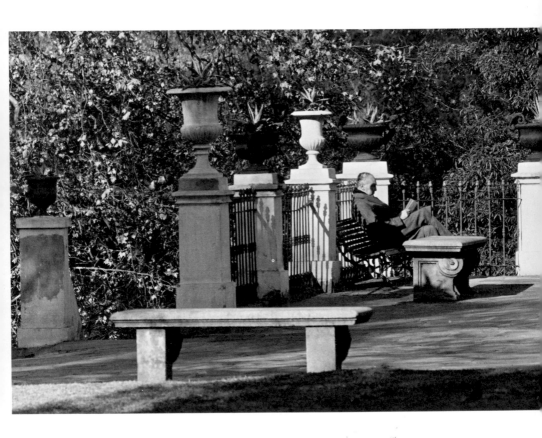

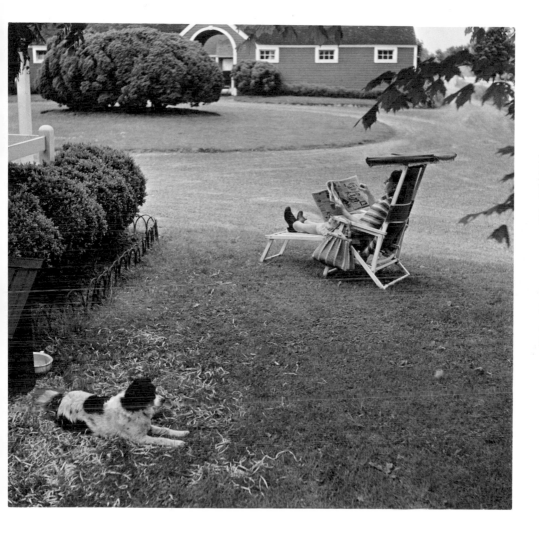

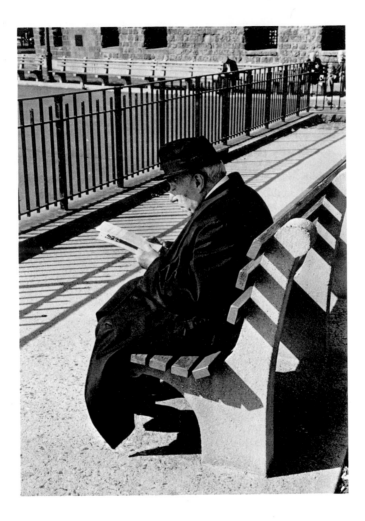

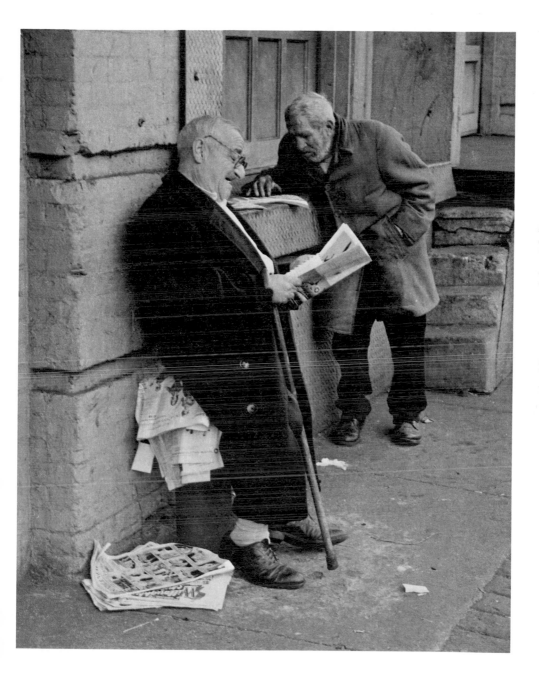

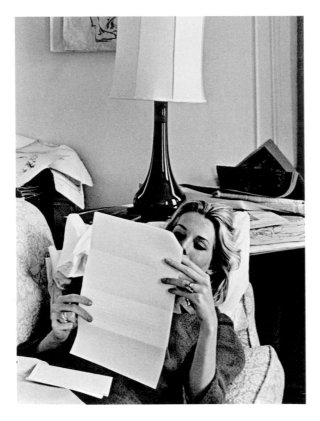

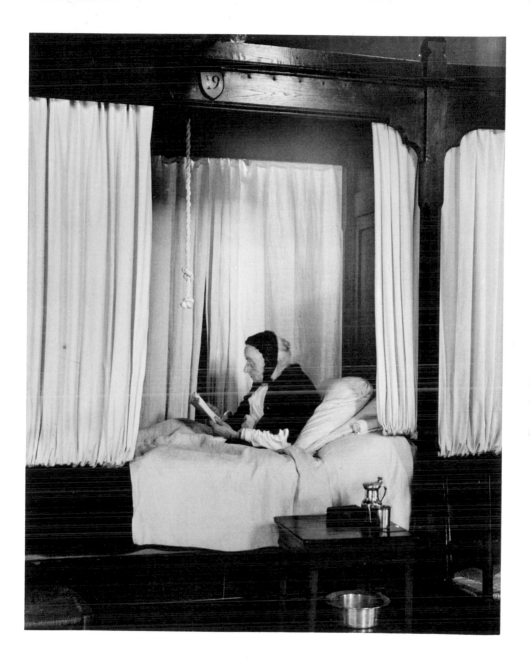

THE PHOTOGRAPHS